The Sight
of Invisible Longing

poems by

Elya Braden

Finishing Line Press
Georgetown, Kentucky

The Sight
of Invisible Longing

"Were you not always distracted by expectation, as though all this were announcing someone to love?"

~Rainer Maria Rilke, *Duino Elegies*,
trans. J.B. Leishman and Stephen Spender

Quietness

Inside this new love, die.
Your way begins on the other side.
Become the sky.
Take an axe to the prison wall.
Escape.
Walk out like someone suddenly born into color.
Do it now.
You're covered with thick cloud.
Slide out the side. Die,
and be quiet. Quietness is the surest sign
that you've died.
Your old life was a frantic running
from silence.

The speechless full moon
comes out now.

~Rumi, *trans.* Coleman Barks

ACKNOWLEDGMENTS

Thank you to Jack Grapes, in whose Method Writing workshop these poems
were birthed as he challenged me to explore the depths of Rilke's *Duino
Elegies* and allow their spirituality and mystery to infuse my writing.

And in gratitude always to Jon, whose creativity inspires and ignites me. In
the words of Rascal Flats: *God blessed the broken road that led me straight to
you.*

Publisher: Leah Huete de Maines
Editor: Christen Kincaid
Cover and Interior Art: Elya Braden
Author Photo: Bader Hower Photography
Cover Design: Elizabeth Maines McCleavy

Order online: www.finishinglinepress.com
                also available on amazon.com

Author inquiries and mail orders:
Finishing Line Press
PO Box 1626
Georgetown, Kentucky 40324
USA

Table of Contents

INTRODUCTION

The ten poems in this collection were inspired by Rainer Maria Rilke's *Duino Elegies*. Other than the first poem, which is based on his Fifth Elegy, they follow the order of the *Duino Elegies*.

PRELUDE

Blood and Bone/Family Dinner the Night Before You Move Out
from *The Wounded Table* by Frida Kahlo

Welcome to the end of the world theatre.
Drawn curtains expose your daily dalliance
with Death. Center stage: your soon-to-be severed
husband and you, his not-so-wife. What has kept you
playing perfect family while even your table
grows feet to run from your Janus-faced platitudes?
Of all the roles you've performed on stage
and board room, wasn't this—devoted wife—
your greatest? Your life, until now,
a drawn breath, as you tightroped
your way to Exodus.

Your husband: chalk-faced. His skewered
head, once inflated with hearth and home,
the certainty of all he owned (his wife,
constant as a chair), now a shrunken toy.
Papier maché monster, his arms huge
with wanting, with fist and threat he sought
to pin his dark-haired beauty
to that museum wall called:
        The Way Things Are Supposed to Be.

He ticks and bleeds. How long has he strung
himself in martyrdom, ghostly chains
of dynamite, ready to explode your world
into winter everlasting? Your children,
schooled in his exclusion waltz:
one-two-three, one-two-three,
stand by him, already loathe
to meet your eye. For who remembers
the vanilla kiss of coffee cake
after it burns in the oven? Your departure:
a residue of ash behind their teeth.

Oh you,
trained from childhood to spill
the teaspoons of your tears in secret
corners, to crawl beneath the stairs,
gashed feline lapping her own blood.
How you grew to love the taste
of hoarded sorrow.

I see how you hide your bristled heart
under bronze breastplate, spackle
swollen eyes with bright concealer, mask
blotted cheeks with rouge.
When will you learn that imperfection
is the bread of fellowship?

       But look—blood drips
beneath your skirt, pools
at your feet. Even the table, wounded
from all you've said or refused
to say, oozes. You, versed in the art
of erasure, will disappear from this picture
tomorrow. Perhaps, in a past life,
you were an osprey or an Angel,
so enamored are you with flight.

Death, dressed in his bleached suit
of rib and scapula, femur and skull, grins
his retort: How do we find meaning
knowing our longest lives sleep
in the maggot womb of the earth? Our bones,
which once paraded haute couture
from Paris runways, will someday
feed the grace of dandelions.

And yet, a doe wanders in
from the garden, not to serve as your last
supper, but as a reminder that roses
will bloom again, a riot of blush
and wine. Yes, the deer may consume
their petaled glory, as your children
once sucked the swell from your breasts,
drew blood and pus with teeth-seeded gums.
And still, those rocking chair nights
glow in memory with the thousand-watt
suns of childhood. Is this your lesson:
to love even love withheld? To trust that Spring
sleeps crusted beneath Winter's shell?

A mother, riven from her children, may dream
of heights and flight, her midnight hair
already climbing Death's gaunt arm.
Let the sigh of the doe remind you
of life's sweet breath. Even the embers
and billowing grit of a raging fire
will sate their hunger, sink
into soil, and green a forest new
with blood and bone.

EVER AFTER

**The Sight of Invisible Longing/You Wake, Alone in Your New
Apartment, Knowing Your Children Are Home with Their Dad**

And to whom shall you pray
when you have bartered the sanctity
of hearth and home for the shivering
pleasures of skin and tongue?
You embrace no Christian ambiguity,
no fable of a prideful angel tumbled
from the mountaintop. Your wandering tribe
scribed Satan as God's gadfly,
gloating gamester flogging man
with knotted losses to test his faith.
How dare we humans demand
that reward and punishment
be meted out according to a cosmology
of clay feet and sacrifice?
Is it not your pride that whispers:
You, like Job, are a paradigm of loss?

Did you think yourself as necessary as milk?
Yes, babies once worshipped at your breast,
but didn't their weaning teach you anything?
Scientists may argue: *nature versus nurture,*
but you know detachment as an acquired taste.
Or that's the lie you tell yourself to silence
that howling infant, *Need,* with its swollen
face and grasping hands.

So many hands clasped your arms.
Were they holding down or carrying aloft?
In dreams of flight, you are a solitary bird,
even a glimpse by some ordinary mortal
hobbles your wings. Do you imagine
the hand of God feeds the thickening waist
of silence stalking your cupboards,
lounging on your favorite couch?

No, you are not so vain, sure
your earthbound sins signify less
than techni-quarks of Time. Even
in nightmare, the thick, purple carpet
of your childhood sanctuary
does not turn into a choking sea
of weeds at the insult of your shoe,
the *Ner Tamid* does not cough
chunks of fire onto your dark curls,
the congregation does not stone you
with thou shalt nots.

Your curse is insignificance.

Look up! See all the absence the sky carries
in her blue rucksack. Each robin sings
her own Psalm. Even the mockingbird
enters in his own measure.
Haven't you, like Jacob, dreamed
a ladder reaching up to Heaven,
resplendent angels climbing
up and down? This is your gift:
the sight of invisible longing.
Even in desolation, the spiny cactus
still bears its armored fruit.
Like the blackberries you once hoarded,
how much sweeter its flesh
rimmed in the coppery tang
of your fingertips' sudden springs.

Drop to your knees. No brambled goat
will save you from the raised knife.
Your children's beds, empty.
Dust mutes their echoing accusations.
What waits beyond sorrow's door?
Bow your head, reverse your tongue,
prepare, at last, to cross its threshold.

The Tulips You Bed/You Bring Home the Hot Guy You Met at a Dance Club

Music thumps the floor, thieves heartbeat, speeds
your blood's gush and pulse, mimics the wind-whip of wings.

Lips trace flames down a ridge of throat.
How like animals we are in our rituals of mating!

What must the Full Buck Moon think of your gyrations?
Taciturn captive in his bunker of clouds, eyes hollow

to your small dramas. Smoke rises. Words dissolve.
You speak with hips and hands, chests thrust forward.

On the hinge of midnight and dawn,
you teeter between drift and desire

in a tatted black camisole's lace. Ice
steams on skin, neck arched, teeth bared.

Only this morning, you attacked the Earth's hide,
raised your trowel like a dagger,

squinted as it bent the sun's poker to stab
your eye. Tears like premonitions.

The tulips you bed in your garden will clang their red
and yellow bells too late for you to heed their warning.

Too long you have ignored the role you insist on playing
in other people's stories. But those who refuse to pay in light

will pay in darkness. You invited a lion to your bed.
Did you imagine you'd wake with a lamb?

The Sentinel Maple outside your window shake their green heads.
They know the beggar bowl of shame you carry.

Did you think you could sink your feet into a riverbank, grow bark,
let the wind whisper your new name in a murmur of leaves?

All your angels have fled. The lion rises, not to leave,
but to strike. He snaps elastic, tears silk, thrusts legs apart.

Neither permission nor forgiveness. His shadow
in your doorway. Your father's hand, again, over your mouth.

Thickening Distance/At an Overnight House Party, You Realize Your Almost-Boyfriend Is an Alcoholic

Harsh spirits: the tyranny of one more mouthful.
You know not the demons who seduce him.
You are not the one who burns in him.
You are only flint to his rock.

Is it his last love, the one who
dangles him by a frayed string?
No, even she is but a shadow
on a cave wall.

His mother's need devoured, flowered
from lymph to lymph like cancer,
gliding through his blood, a gondolier
singing love songs in foreign tongues.

She folded messages in the cracks of his walls,
indecipherable prayers he attempts to answer
in fevered couplings with any She
who vibrates in a familiar key.

How this new configuration of shoulder
and knee, elbow and waist, moss and loam
promises a litany of tomorrows if only
he could find the path!

Wandering your forest, ripe with pomegranate
and fig, he can't ignore the desiccation
of his fields. Green and verdant,
jealousy vines his torso, vises his lungs.

His hand shakes as he raises another glass.
He sees you as through a shard of broken mirror
grafted in his eye. His desire drowned.
No more lighthouse or buoy,

You are but a bobbing log he'd shove
beneath the water to hold himself afloat.
Don't we all long to kill the giant in whose presence
we feel like scuttling ants, too busy to see the sky?

Who among us could believe
that we were born for such greatness,
that the reaching hand intends
not to strike us down, but lift us up?

You, who once sailed through rough waters
over uncharted seas, returning with bounties
of silver and gold, now huddle by the shore
as he swims away.

Is this what his mother taught him:
to enjoy the confusion his thickening
distance draws on the face
of the woman he once wooed?

Your skin still jasmines the breeze as the stars
pinhole the night with their thousand-year songs.
The ocean spills its indigo ink on the page
of the beach: an ode to love.

But he has tumbled over the edge,
into the backwash of his drained bottle.
Glassed in. Deaf to all but the whine
of his constant thirst.

אשוב

Night Soil/You Wear a Strap-On for a *Friend*

Since Genesis, our history transcribed
as a binary tale. Out of Chaos, light & dark,
day & night. Out of Adam, Eve. Out of apple,
good & evil. But what of Lilith, Adam's first wife,
molded not from rib, but earth, like him?
Legend tells she refused to lie beneath him,
nor he beneath her, and it was not good.
She uttered the Divine name, flew into the air
and fled the Garden. Her name stricken
from the record.

Were you born, like Eve, knowing how to be
a woman with a man, or merely groomed
to statued resistance by father, by brother?
You can scour their fingerprints from your skin,
purge the crime scene of your body with
floral douches, Ex-lax, and walk the aisle
in snowy alencon lace and seed pearls,
but just as DNA inscribes ancestry
on cheek bones, the slant of eye or cast
of skin, so your future is written in your past.

What were the seeds of your undoing?
The Rabbi's missed instruction for you
to circle your husband seven times under
the Chuppah? No, dip further into your pool
of yesterdays, smell the dust beneath your brother's
bed, feel the slick pages of his naughty magazines
on your naked knees, your eyes breathing images
of girl on girl while your busy finger spins
the record of your desire.

Now you, like Lilith, have fled the Garden,
what isn't possible? After years of nights
ringing pleasure's bell swaddled in fantasies
of femme-soft fingers and tongues,
being a woman with a woman
was a skin you eeled into as easily
as you once donned pillows, wig
and polyester to play a fat, old British shrew.
And voilà, by closing night, that chapter,
too, is through.

***

Love wears a revolving face. Eyes
now brown, now hazel, now blue.
Hair now auburn, umber or gravel.
Clean-shaven Wednesday, bearded Saturday.
A pledge of time and body parts,
hours dealt to the highest bidder.

Life a series of dress rehearsals:
no intermission, no script,
and no finale, only endless costume
changes. Your face in a cracked mirror
under a weary light. Your lipstick
violating the boundaries of your mouth.
One stubborn eyebrow higher
than its mate. Every line informed
by past lives you were born forgetting.

You can tear or cackle on demand,
but with every new mask, you disappear
another boulevard, another alley,
another high-rise in the city of yourself
until you're wandering a borderless
country and you've lost the word
            for *No*.

***

Enter *Scene One*: three years past,
a conference of wisdom seekers: you,
neophyte; He, group leader. Who has not
climbed truth's mountain, goat-sure
that the guru crossed-legged at the peak
cavorts with Angels, bends God's ear?

***

Scene Two: curtains rise to present day,
a weekend getaway to the conference city.
Dinner with your group leader, now *friend*
via a cyberspace trail of email. As your marriage
unraveled, he listened, counseled, *soothed*.
How could his intentions not wear feathers?

You, too, play God, dividing the world:
truth or lie, table or chair, kosher or trayf,
friend or lover, safety or sex.
Yet you're still blind to the lechery
behind a *friend's* smile, his silvered ask:
Wanna come in for a nightcap?
Father, brother, employer, thief.
Haven't you learned that violation
already hides under your bed,
chews the shoes in your closet?

When he says, *Let's play a game,*
it sings of childhood puppet shows
in felt, feathers, and ribbons, not
the synch of a leather strap between
your legs, around your hips. You never laid
Tefillin after your Bat Mitzvah nor dreamed
of playing man to a man.
You are Libra, not Ram;
Air, not Earth; Kali, not Shiva.

***

The fumes of night-soil revolt you.
You will not wash them
from your skin. You will not unfurl
this tale to your confidantes.
You will not scratch a fresh notch
in your belt of conquest. Instead,
you will brick another room
in your mansion of disremembering
as you watch the hour hand creep
past midnight, past one, past two.

The Virgin's Promise/You Give Your Crush from Acting Class a Second Chance After He Stands You Up

How you thirsted for the pomegranate of your youth.
Like her, you carried your sweetness in an inner sea:
sealed, sectioned, secret. You, too, have been broken
open, bled your red rage. The apple may have stolen
sweet pomegranate's place in Earth's first garden,
but she is as ancient and abiding as myth.
Ruby-leathered child of Aphrodite,
femininity revealed in her darkening blush,
the spilling of her uncountable seeds.
She is suckle, stain, pillage, curse. Daughter's
temptation, mother's agony, promise of spring.

***

                    .... Bottle-fed by a mother all
elbows and smoke, clocks and *Stop!* you grew ignorant
of the alphabet of touch. You were arrow, destination,
trekking your father's footprints, scaling peaks
of paltry air like Icarus in strapped-on wings,
eager for sun. But melt we always do. The Angels
refuse to share the sky. Success, that winsome seductress,
tempted you with the wiles of Delilah: *What is the secret
of your strength?* she badgered. You lied and lied and lied
again, tied yourself in knots, broke free. The truth is
you have shorn your own hair, bared your naked throat,
bound your thighs into trousers, all for some elusive
seat at the table. Die, you must, to be reborn,
that is the virgin's promise. Your future a wheel, *Shuva*,
turn and return, your tomorrows written in your past.

***

Now, you reverse the clock, plunge into acting
classes, wear your *beginner's mind*. You girl your hair
back into tumble and flow. Is Joy a bubble
beneath your breastbone or a lump in the throat?

Between notes and takes and costume changes,
you reorder your life into stanzas.
Unlike Adam, this time you don't rush to name
every creature outside your skin. Instead, you cast
your net upon your inner shores, tune ears
to the thump and swoosh of crimson-fisted muscle,
the pepper spray of grief gutting your breath,
the tickle and sing of heat down there when He
walks in.

***

A second chance at a first impression? Married
when you'd first met, you now wander the wilderness
of *After*, self-exiled from the kingdom of hearth and home.
Possibility fans your brow with her beating of wings.
You are leafing, a tree in full sap, your limbs dripping
with *Yeses*. Fate, whose humor fattens on banana peels
and lost lottery tickets, clashes you two like cymbals:
once, twice, thrice. So, when He stumbles, tangled
in dreams and distance, is it the self-deprecating humility
of his apology, the memory of his eyes—that particular
blue of sun on Sound—or your deference to *B'shert,
it was meant to be,* that makes you laugh and set
another date? How much easier to forgive with your toes
coddled in warm sand. Would we all grow kinder
living by the shore?

exhale of wings

Songbird Broken/Singing Only for Auditions, You Lose Your Joy in Music

Once you were sparkle, chiffon and sequins.
In smoky jazz clubs, you jeweled the night,
bantered with bar flies, paid tribute to stars
of scale and pine—Cole and Ella, Peggy, Nina.
Under a happy moon, you floated on the calm
waters of *Enough*, content to trail your fingers
in reflected glory.

Ha!

Those who know you, know better,
know the truth of your yard dog hunger,
know your tapeworm of shame,
know the fevered bite of your tarantella,
know the stumbled marathon you treadmill,
know the whip of the beast's footfalls,
know with every victory you notch the marker higher,
know your satisfaction taps its foot behind the next door,
know you rewrite history through the cataract of nostalgia.

How your song, splintered with wanting,
has startled in your throat, cartwheels sunk
in sand. Every note a scorecard of insufficiency.
That careless F sharp swirling in the mist of morning's
shower now screeches on Inquisition's rack,
catgut stretched to dog whimper, to glass shatter.
On waves of ego, your ancient rowboat—Pride—
tosses, cracks, leaks.

But weren't the Angels there,
luminous, patient, poised to intercede?
How could you know? You'd fled the chambered halls
of vaulted ceilings and stained glass, scorned
the annual congregation in their Fall finery,
flaunting the piety of their Fast,

paying a premium for prime placement—
a designated parking spot, a seat on the altar.
You'd chased God through too many temples
before abandoning your quest.

What if everything you need is already within you?
You stare into the mirror, but no one stares back.
Gone, your wisdom of *Before*. Gone, your aura of *Heaven*,
the light of a thousand suns dawning in your newborn eyes.
Gone, the knowing of your two-year-old son:
> *Mommy, don't eat my toes!*
> *They're special because God made them.*
Surely, you must have glimpsed the Angels then,
felt the exhale of their wings, or cocked your head
at the waft of myrrh and snow. Or were you too busy
tallying the riches of your neighbor's field?
Even breath, that ever-present gift, you sipped
through pinched lips, your tongue thick
with the after-musk of your childhood blanket,
thin protector from the shadow in your doorway.

Where is the key to unlock transformation's gate?
Not in the arms of your young lover
nor in the swoon of his kisses.
Night after night, you take to your balcony,
baptize yourself in rain. God, a fairytale
spun in Sunday school. Your only savior—
the calculable distance between rail and concrete.

Would a miracle wear a face or simply whisper:
Retreat? Who would you be without the striving?
To stop and let the wolf devour you.
To sing for no purpose or prize.
To open your mouth and release
> a murmuration of notes,
> music delighting in flight.

blade of faith

Shehecheyanu/You Escape to Israel on Thanksgiving After Your Children Choose to Feast with Their Father

So brief your courtship with Jerusalem,
yet every Spring, with your tribe,
you have promised to return
to her kneeling dawns, her wailing dusks,
her chattering alleys baked
in cumin, turmeric and za'atar.
You are a folded prayer waiting
to be spoken by the Divine.

Is it the Shofar blast of *Home*,
the surge and *whoosh* of the collective
womb that summons you to *Ha'aretz*?
Or are you another desperate servant
fleeing to Samarra, imagining you can outrun
Death, the death of *Mother* in eyes
that stare beyond and past you?

In flight, signs are everywhere. Even
the sky holds the story of your name
in its blue mouth, speaks through a
bearded rabbinic student, his lips
versed in ancient texts. Elohim and Yahweh
divided, mated, your spirit woven
of many hands, all reaching out to God.
Why have you believed this deity, this
him/her/it, as distant as the clouds when
the sky always lowered her invisible face
to Earth, breathed flowers into exaltation?
See—even the spiny sabras, drunk
on a mere trickle of *mayim*, lark
their bright song in red and fuchsia flashes.

How long you watched from the sidelines
of your life, ignoring Death's insistent question:
Is this all there is? Now, you descend
into your present-past, bow under
a relentless sun, and press your lips
to black tarmac. If your chestnut curls
mark you as stranger amidst the flutter
of headscarves and black hats,
you neither know nor care. Instead,
you thicken your tongue, gutter your throat
and chant:
> [1]*Baruch atah, Adonai Eloheinu, Melech haolam,*
> *shehecheyanu, v'kiy'manu, v'higiyanu laz'man hazeh.*

---

1 Blessed are You, Adonai our God, Sovereign of all, who has kept us alive, sustained us, and brought us to this season.

Fallow Time/At a Spiritual Retreat in the Galilee, You Search the Wilderness for Meaning

How long have you wandered
this wilderness:
            no compass, no watch, no map?
Your thoughts burst in,
steaming geysers greening the desert.

Who are you to compare
your paltry minutes to the forty years
your ancestors were banished
from this promised land?

Do you fear your lack of faith
will condemn you, as theirs did,
even here at the base of Mount Gilboa?

Once, the Christians named
this valley *Armageddon*, destined
for the penultimate battle
between good and evil.

You, too, imagined destiny
drew you here, but why?
Everywhere you run, the empty bell
of your life clangs: *Fill me! Fill me!*

What are you here to tell me?
You interrogate a barren terebinth tree.

Slow down, look:
this tree, its trunk blistered with gallnuts,
growths sprung from aphid stings,
its bark mottled in deprivation.

What do you know of loss?
The ghosts of Yad Va'shem swathe you
in the smoke of six million candles snuffed.

Hallways of voices on a forever loop,
a tell of shoes, a tumble of books, a toss
of teeth. Better to have been this terebinth,
leeching life from rock and dust

than to remember you once swore
loyalty to Fatherland
as you are torn from home,
herded to train to camp to shower.

Untellable.

Here, in Jezreel, Death speaks
        in many tongues:
the *thwip* and *pock* of gunshots,
roving packs of feral dogs,
viper bite, scorpion sting.

Thirst. Loneliness.

Yesterday, on the Northern border,
you watched soldiers march in single file,
twenty paces or more apart.
Why? You asked your guide.

Below, the roar and suck of sea
foamed the mouth of Rosh Hanikra.
Above, the whine of tension wire,
the bobbing shell of gondola
white against cerulean sky.

Sweat frizzed your hair, salted
your lip. Your socks wilted.
So, if one of them steps on a land mine,
he explained, *the others will be safe.*

Surely, they know why they're here,
born into this ancient land
where Adam once gave name
to horse, dove, goat, fish, snake.

Under this old sky, *Chosen*
is an earthen jar, tall, unwieldy,
too heavy for *you* to carry.

You expect no biblical deity
to set fire to the ground,
to wake you from your dream,
to call you to some higher purpose.

Look again, the tree. Its leaves
winter-vanquished yes, but see:
there and there—new buds, barely visible.

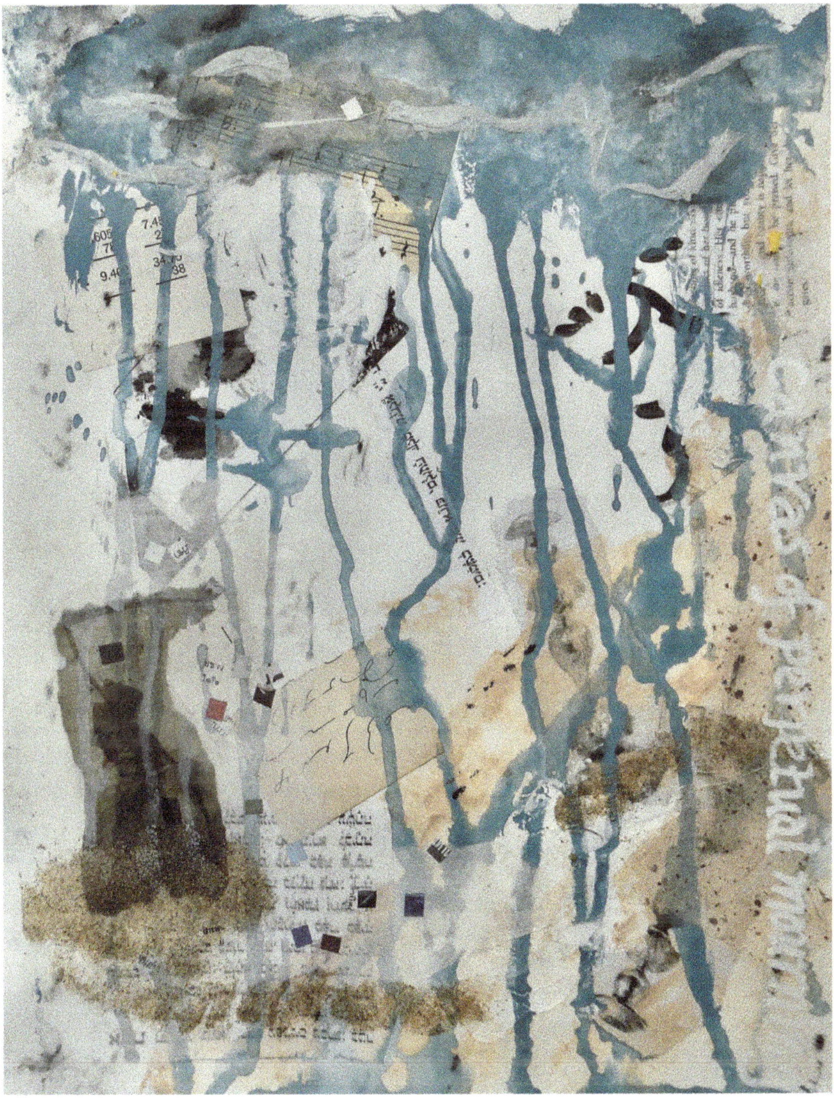
of Perpetual

Sea of Lamentation/You Return to Seattle to Celebrate Chanukah Alone

You dream of the whispering cisterns
of Masada, that clutch of freedom fighters
on a mountaintop, refusing to forsake
Yahweh, the one true God.

Death mounts the twisted goat trails,
breeches the raised walls,
reclaims his bitter spoils.

Would you have arched your neck
under the blade of faith,
or snatched a child's hand and fled?

For millennia, your *People of the Book*
have kissed the hem of its velvet mantel,
unscrolled its hand-hewn skins,
grasped the silver-tooled *yad*, hand
of God, pointed their way through
seasoned stories of persecution.

Oh, how we burn.
Oh, how we rise.

Is this what we were Chosen for—
to bathe in a sea of lamentation,
to ever mourn our losses
instead of gathering into our basket
of astonishment each glint of light
on rippled glass, each crowning
newborn, each flower struggling
between the cobblestones?

Yes, our prayer book warms us
as a ragbag quilt of odes, homage
to eternal gratitude. *Barach ata adonai*—
Blessed are you, Lord, our God—
we chant, with one ear cocked for
the hoofbeats of Destruction tearing
up the road, hellbent for our homes.

Why is disaster easier to believe than hope?

***

Heading down the mountain, you arrive at the Sea
of Death, pool of a thousand million tears.
In Arabic, she is known as the Sea of Lot,
but wasn't it Lot's *wife* who turned to salt?

Was it regret and longing that turned
her head, or compassion: a glimmer
that evil could be redeemed or the tug
of her elder daughters, left behind,
on her maternal cord?

And what of her two youngest girls,
captive in the cave with their father,
bearing his children? Better to be struck
into salt than witness that.

It's been said that to have children
is to allow your heart to wander outside
your body. Yours has wandered so far away
your chest echoes with the slosh of seawater.

Their father emails you photos of their exploits.
Is it a kindness or a curse to see the stories
of their lives distilled to silent pixels?

***

You wake to Seattle, your city of salt, the sky
a canvas of perpetual mourning, clouds fisting
above your head, turning day into night,
night into unseeing, the stars obliterated,
the moon exiled to a great beyond.

Each night of Chanukah, in the dim silence
of your living room, you light another candle,
intone the blessings but sing no songs.
You have no *dreidels* to twirl, no *gelt* to eat.
Pariah to friends you once familied—
what use a mother without children?

Remember Lot's wife. You walk a new path.
Do not look back.

Elya Braden was born a poet, singer/actor and artist, but took an 18-year hiatus from her creative life so she could play "Let's Make A Deal" as a corporate securities lawyer and entrepreneur. After serving as General Counsel of a public Internet company in the late '90's, she retired from law at the end of 2000. Elya went on to create a networking group for experienced women lawyers, to launch a new business, and to serve on corporate and non-profit boards. Elya also returned to her passion for singing in jazz clubs, cabarets and musicals, as well as acting in plays, independent films and commercials.

Elya is now a poet and mixed-media artist living in Channel Islands Harbor in Ventura County, CA with her husband, the brilliant short story writer, artist and creativity consultant, Jon Pearson, and their recently adopted cat, Phoebe. She is Assistant Editor of *Gyroscope Review*. Elya has been a featured reader at Tasty Words, Library Girl, the Rapp Saloon, Cobalt Poets (on Zoom) and Beatnik Cafe (on Zoom). Her work has been published in *Calyx, Prometheus Dreaming, Rattle Poets Respond, Sequestrum, Sheila-Na-Gig Online, The Coachella Review* and elsewhere. Her poems have received *The Ekphrastic Review*'s Fantastic Ekphrastic Award, Editor's Choice awards, and have been nominated for the Pushcart Prize, Best of the Net and Best New Poets. Her first chapbook, *Open The Fist*, was released in 2020 by Finishing Line Press.

Following her success publishing her poetry in literary journals and magazines, Elya created and led workshops for other writers on How to Get Published. Elya now leads a nonprofit, HaGomel (www. hagomel.org), which provides expressive arts programs for women who have experienced sexual trauma to support their emotional and psychological healing. Visit Elya online at www.elyabraden.com.

www.ingramcontent.com/pod-product-compliance
Lightning Source LLC
Chambersburg PA
CBHW050029090426
42734CB00021B/3476